10-30-16

This is a great milestone for you Philip! May today be a special and memorable one! God bless and guide you through your life.

Love,
Grandma and Grandpa [signature]

The Illustrated
Bible for
Little Ones

HARVEST HOUSE PUBLISHERS
EUGENE, OREGON

The Illustrated Bible for Little Ones

©2015 (North America) International Publishing
Services Pty Ltd. Sydney Australia.
www.ipsoz.com, External Markets © NPP Ltd Bath
Written by J. Emmerson- Hicks
Illustrations by Netscibes

Published by Harvest House Publishers
Eugene, Oregon 97402
www.harvesthousepublishers.com

ISBN 978-0-7369-6552-1

15 16 17 18 19 20 21 22 23 / IPS / 10 9 8 7 6 5 4 3 2 1

Contents

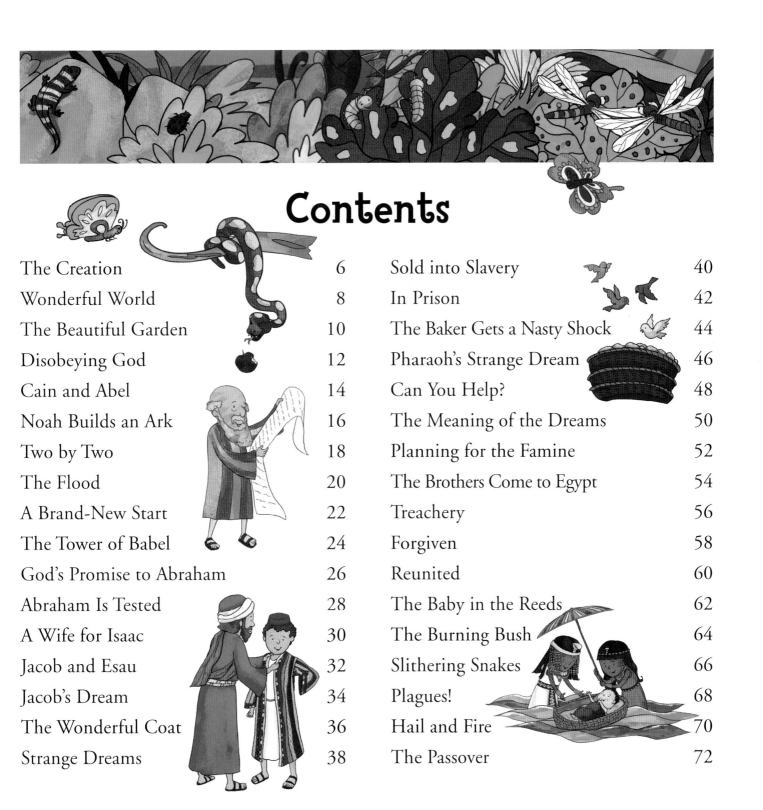

The Creation
(Genesis 1)

In the beginning, there was nothing at all—no sunshine, no land, no animals, no people. Can you even imagine that? Absolutely nothing!

Then God created heaven and earth, but everything was still covered in darkness, so God said, "Let there be light," and there was light! God called the light day and the darkness night, and that was the very first day and the very first night.

In the days that followed, God separated the water from dry land and covered the land with beautiful plants and trees and lovely green grass. He made the sun to shine during the day and the moon and stars to light up the night sky.

Wonderful World
(Genesis 1-2)

God filled the seas with enormous whales and bright, shiny fish, leaping dolphins and wobbly jellyfish. Then he filled the skies with beautiful birds of every color imaginable. Next he made animals of all shapes and sizes—spotted cheetahs that could run like the wind, slow tortoises that carried their homes on their backs, huge elephants with long trunks, and many, many more.

Last of all God made man and woman and told them to take care of this wonderful world and all the living creatures on it.

God was pleased with all he had made and done, so on the seventh day, he rested and made that day a special day, a day to stop working and give thanks.

The Beautiful Garden
(Genesis 2)

God made Adam, the very first man, in his own image. He created for him the beautiful Garden of Eden, a marvelous paradise filled with green grass, colorful plants, and wonderful trees. God told Adam that he might help himself to fruit from any of these trees except for one: the tree of knowledge. There were still plenty of other wonderful things for him to eat.

God brought all the animals and birds to Adam for him to name. None of the animals were like him, and Adam was lonely, so God created a woman, Eve, to be his special friend and companion. They had no clothes to wear, but that didn't bother them at all.

Disobeying God
(Genesis 3)

Of all the animals, the most cunning was the snake. One day the snake said to Eve, "Why don't you eat from the tree of knowledge? The fruit is delicious and won't harm you! God doesn't want you to eat it because it will make you wise like him. Take a bite!"

The fruit looked so delicious that Eve picked some and offered some to Adam too, and they both ate it. At once they realized they were naked and tried to cover themselves with leaves.

God was very angry. He cursed the snake and sent Adam and Eve away. He told them that from now on they would have to work hard to make their own food and clothes. Then he placed an angel with a flaming sword to stand guard at the entrance to the garden.

13

Cain and Abel
(Genesis 4)

Adam and Eve had two sons. Cain was a farmer who worked in the fields and Abel was a shepherd. One day Cain and Abel both brought offerings to God. Abel brought the very best meat he could, and God was pleased, but he was not so pleased with the crops that Cain had brought.

Cain was so jealous of his brother that he went out with him into the fields and killed him in a fit of anger. When God asked where Abel was, Cain answered rudely, "How should I know? Am I my brother's keeper?"

But God saw Abel's blood on the ground and was angry. He punished Cain and sent him far away from his home and family.

Noah Builds an Ark
(Genesis 6)

Many years passed, and soon there were lots of people in the world. They were becoming more and more wicked, and this made God very sad. He made up his mind to send a terrible flood to destroy everything he had created.

But there was one good man on earth who loved and obeyed God. His name was Noah, and he had three sons. God told Noah to build an enormous boat—an ark—so that he and his family might be saved along with two of every living creature.

People thought Noah was really silly for building a boat in the middle of the land, and they made fun of him. But he ignored them because he trusted God.

Two by Two
(Genesis 6-7)

Noah built the amazing boat out of cypress wood. It had lots of rooms inside and was three decks high. God told him exactly how it should be made and how big it should be. It took Noah and his three sons a long, long time to finish it.

When the ark was finished, Noah, his wife, his sons, and their wives loaded it with food for themselves and the animals. Then God sent the animals to the ark, two by two—one male and one female of every kind of animal and bird that lived upon the earth or flew in the skies.

Once they were all safely in, God closed the door behind them.

The Flood
(Genesis 7)

Now it began to rain. And how it rained! Water poured down from the skies and covered all the land. Every living creature was drowned. All the towns and cities were washed away. But the ark and its precious cargo floated free on a world of water.

A Brand-New Start
(Genesis 7-9)

For forty days and forty nights, it rained. Then, at last, it stopped! After a while the floodwaters began to go down. Noah sent out a dove, and when it returned with an olive leaf in its beak, Noah knew that the flood was over. The trees were growing again.

Then it was time for Noah and the animals to leave the ark. Noah was filled with gratitude because God promised him that he would never again send such a dreadful flood. God even put a beautiful rainbow in the sky to remind everyone of this promise.

The Tower of Babel
(Genesis 11)

To begin with, the world had only one language so everyone could understand everyone else. There came a time when some of Noah's descendants decided to build a city. It would be famous throughout the land and have a tower reaching to the heavens.

But God feared they were becoming too proud and vain, so he made them unable to understand one other. Soon a great babble of voices was heard. Everyone was speaking in a different language. No one could understand anyone else!

In all the confusion, building stopped, and the people scattered far and wide. The tower became known as the Tower of Babel.

God's Promise to Abraham
(Genesis 12-13)

Abraham was a good man who trusted in God. God asked Abraham to go to another land. He promised to bless him and to make him the father of a great nation. Abraham had a good home where he was happy, but when God told him to leave, he took his wife, Sarah, his nephew, Lot, and all his servants and set out for Canaan.

God told him that he would have too many descendants to count—as many as the stars in the sky—and that the land of Canaan would one day belong to them.

Even though Abraham and his wife were very old and hadn't had a child, Abraham trusted in God.

Abraham Is Tested
(Genesis 22)

Abraham and his wife, Sarah, were very old before they had the baby that God had promised them. Isaac grew up to be a fine young boy, and his parents loved him dearly. But one day God decided to test Abraham by saying that he must offer the boy as a sacrifice!

Abraham was heartbroken, but he trusted God, and so he prepared to do as he had been told. But as he lifted up his knife, an angel cried, "Abraham! Do not harm the boy! I know now that you love God with all your heart for you were willing to give up your son."

God sent a ram to be sacrificed instead and told Abraham that he would bless him and his family because of his faith.

A Wife for Isaac
(Genesis 24)

Years later Abraham sent his most trusted servant back to his homeland to find a wife for his beloved son. When the servant reached his master's hometown, he prayed to God to send a sign.

Before he had finished praying, beautiful Rebekah came out to draw water from the well. When the servant asked if he might have a drink, she offered her jar straightaway and then hurried to draw water for his camels too.

This was the sign the servant had asked for! He thanked God and then explained his mission to Rebekah, and when her father was asked, it was agreed that she should become Isaac's wife. When Isaac and Rebekah finally met, they fell in love with one another instantly!

Jacob and Esau
(Genesis 25-27)

When Rebekah was old, she and Isaac had twins. Esau, the firstborn (who was rather hairy), became a great hunter, while Jacob spent more time at home. One day Esau agreed to give Jacob his birthright in exchange for a plate of stew—just because he was so hungry!

When Isaac was very old and nearly blind, he wished to give his blessing to his eldest son. Rebekah, who was especially fond of Jacob, helped Jacob tie goatskins around his arms so he would be hairy like his brother. Believing him to be Esau, his father gave Jacob his blessing to be in charge of the family when he died!

Esau was so angry that he wanted to kill his brother. Jacob had to leave home for his own safety.

Jacob's Dream
(Genesis 28)

Jacob was traveling to the house of his uncle. On the way he stopped for the night. He lay down on the hard ground to sleep and had a strange dream. He saw a stairway resting on the earth with its top reaching to heaven. Angels were walking up and down it.

At the very top stood God. He said, "I am the Lord, the God of your father Abraham and the God of Isaac. I will give you and your descendants this land. They will be like the dust of the earth, and you will spread to the west and the east, to the north and the south. I will watch over you wherever you go, and I will bring you back to this land. I will not leave you until I have done what I have promised."

35

The Wonderful Coat
(Genesis 37)

Jacob lived in Canaan. He had twelve sons, but Joseph was his favorite. To show Joseph just how much he loved him, Jacob had a wonderful coat made for him—a long-sleeved robe covered with colorful embroidery.

His brothers were jealous, but what really angered them was when Joseph began telling them of the dreams he had had…

Strange Dreams
(Genesis 37)

"Last night I dreamed we were collecting sheaves of grain when suddenly my sheaf stood up straight, and yours all bowed down before it," Joseph told his brothers.

"What are you saying?" growled the brothers. "That you're going to rule over us someday? Go away!"

Joseph had another dream where the sun and moon and eleven stars were bowing down before him. Even his father was cross when he heard about the latest dream.

"Do you really think that your mother and I and your brothers are going to bow down to you? Don't get too big for your boots!"

But Jacob did wonder to himself about what Joseph's dream might mean.

39

Sold into Slavery
(Genesis 37)

Joseph's brothers had had enough! With the fabulous coat and now these dreadful dreams, they felt the time had come to get rid of their annoying brother.

One day when they were out in the fields, the brothers set upon Joseph, tore off his multicolored coat, and threw him in a deep pit. Then they sat down nearby to eat, deaf to his cries for help!

Soon they saw a caravan of Ishmaelite traders passing by on their camels on their way to Egypt. Quick as a flash they decided to sell Joseph to the traders.

Then they took his beautiful coat and ripped it into pieces. They killed a goat, smeared the coat with the blood, and told their poor father that Joseph had been killed by a wild animal!

In Prison
(Genesis 39-40)

In Egypt Joseph was sold to one of Pharaoh's officials, a man named Potiphar. Joseph was clever and hardworking, and soon Potiphar placed him in charge of his whole household. But Potiphar's wife told lies about Joseph to her husband, and poor Joseph found himself thrown into jail!

Sometime later Pharaoh's wine steward and his chief baker angered Pharaoh and also ended up in prison. One night they had strange dreams. Joseph told them God would help him explain the dreams.

The wine steward went first. "In my dream I squeezed the grapes from three branches on a vine into Pharaoh's cup."

Joseph told him that within three days Pharaoh would forgive him, and he asked the steward to remember him.

The Baker Gets a Nasty Shock
(Genesis 40)

Now the baker was anxious to tell his dream too. "On my head were three baskets of bread," he said, "but birds were eating Pharaoh's pastries."

Joseph was sad. He really didn't want to have to tell the baker what his dream meant. "Within three days Pharaoh will cut off your head, and the birds will eat your flesh," he said reluctantly.

Things turned out just as Joseph had foretold, for in three days it was Pharaoh's birthday, and on that day he pardoned the wine steward and gave him back his job, but he executed the chief baker!

The wine steward forgot all about Joseph, though.

Pharaoh's Strange Dream
(Genesis 41)

Two years passed by. Then one night, Pharaoh, the king of Egypt, had a strange dream. He was standing by the Nile when out of the river came seven fat and healthy cows to graze among the reeds. Then seven other cows came up out of the Nile. These cows were ugly and thin. They ate up the fat cows and yet looked just as thin and sickly as before!

Pharaoh had another dream. In this dream seven healthy heads of grain were growing on a single stalk. Then seven more heads of grain sprouted. These were thin and scorched by the wind. But the thin heads of grain swallowed up the seven healthy, full heads!

Can You Help?
(Genesis 41)

In the morning Pharaoh was worried. He sent for all the magicians and wise men of Egypt, but no one could tell him what his strange dreams might mean.

It was only then that the wine steward remembered Joseph. The slave was brought before mighty Pharaoh, who asked him to explain his dreams.

"I cannot do it," Joseph humbly replied to Pharaoh, "but God will be able to explain."

And so Pharaoh told Joseph all about his dreams.

49

The Meaning of the Dreams
(Genesis 41)

Joseph told Pharaoh, "The two dreams are really one and the same. The seven cows and the seven heads of grain are seven years. The land will be blessed with seven years of healthy crops and fine harvests, but they will be followed by seven years of dreadful famine. You will need to plan very carefully to prepare."

Pharaoh spoke to his advisors and then turned to Joseph and said, "Clearly you are the man for the job! I will put you in charge of my land, and you will be second only to me in all of Egypt!"

With that Pharaoh put his own signet ring on Joseph's finger, placed a gold chain around his neck, and dressed him in fine clothes.

Planning for the Famine
(Genesis 41)

Joseph traveled throughout the land in a fine chariot to make sure that food was put aside for the hard times ahead. Just as he had foretold, for seven years the crops grew better than ever before, and so much grain was put away in big storehouses that he gave up counting it!

After seven years the famine began. When people began to run out of food, Joseph opened up the storehouses and sold the grain. No one in Egypt went hungry. In fact there was so much food that people from other countries came to buy it because the famine was bad everywhere.

The Brothers Come to Egypt
(Genesis 42-43)

Joseph's brothers were among those who came to buy grain because the famine had been bad in Canaan too. Only his youngest brother, Benjamin, had stayed behind. The brothers bowed down before Joseph. With his golden chain and fine clothes, they did not recognize him at all!

Joseph wanted to see if his brothers had changed, and so he decided to test them. He agreed to let them go back home with grain, but only if they returned with their youngest brother.

Jacob did not want to let Benjamin go, but in the end he had to agree, and so all the brothers returned to Egypt.

Treachery
(Genesis 43-44)

The test wasn't over. Joseph had his servants feed the brothers and then sent them on their way with more grain, but not before hiding a silver cup in Benjamin's sack.

The brothers were traveling home when guards came and dragged them back to the palace.

"Thieves!" shouted Joseph. "You repay my kindness by stealing!"

"There must be some mistake!" cried the horrified brothers, but when the guards checked, there was the silver cup in Benjamin's sack!

The brothers fell to their knees. "My lord," they cried, "take any one of us, but do not take Benjamin! That would break his father's heart."

57

Forgiven
(Genesis 45)

At this Joseph knew that his brothers really had changed. They cared so much for their little brother and for how upset their father would be that any one of them would have given himself up to save Benjamin.

Crying tears of joy, Joseph went to hug them and told them who he really was. He told them not to feel too bad about what had happened because it had all been part of God's plan. "I was sent to rule in Egypt so that you would not starve in Canaan!" he said.

At first they could hardly believe that this great man was their long lost brother, but when they did, they were filled with joy because they had spent many years feeling sorry for what they had done.

59

Reunited
(Genesis 45-46)

Now it was time to tell Jacob the good news. When the brothers returned and said that his beloved son Joseph was not only alive and well, but governor of all Egypt, old Jacob could hardly believe his ears! But when he saw all the fine gifts that Joseph had sent him, he had to believe his eyes.

Jacob gathered up all his belongings, his herds, and flocks, and he and all his family traveled to Egypt, where Pharaoh had promised them good farmland.

Joseph came to meet his father in a great chariot, and the reunion was just as happy and as emotional as you could possibly imagine!

The Baby in the Reeds
(Exodus 2)

What could Moses' mother do? Her baby boy was healthy and beautiful, but the ruler of Egypt had ordered all Hebrew baby boys killed! So she wrapped him in a shawl, placed him in a basket, and then lowered him into the water among the reeds.

By chance the king's daughter found the basket. "This must be one of the Hebrew babies," she said softly as she picked him up and cradled him gently.

Moses' sister was watching and offered to fetch someone to nurse the baby. The princess agreed, and Miriam darted off to find her mother, who then looked after Moses until he was old enough for the princess to take him to the palace.

63

The Burning Bush
(Exodus 3-4)

Moses grew up in the palace. When he became angry at how the Egyptians treated his fellow Hebrews, he left Egypt and became a shepherd. One day while tending his sheep, he noticed that a nearby bush was on fire, yet the leaves were not burning. As he stepped closer, he heard God speaking to him!

God said, "I will rescue my people and bring them out of Egypt and into the Promised Land. You must tell Pharaoh to free them!"

Moses was scared, but God would not listen to his excuses. He told Moses that he would be with him and sent him back to Egypt. He also sent his brother, Aaron, to help him.

Slithering Snakes
(Exodus 5-7)

Moses and Aaron told Pharaoh, "The God of Israel asks you to let his people go." Pharaoh could not believe their nerve. In fact he was so angry that he made the slaves work even harder!

Moses and Aaron tried again. Pharaoh demanded some proof of God. Aaron threw his staff to the ground, and it was transformed into a fearsome snake! But the king's magicians performed sorcery, and when they threw their staffs on the ground, they too turned into snakes. Even though Aaron's snake swallowed up all the other snakes, the king's heart was hardened, and he would not let the Hebrews go.

Plagues!
(Exodus 7-11)

Then God sent a series of plagues—each more terrible than the last—upon the Egyptians.

First he changed the waters of the Nile into blood so that all the fish died and the air stank. Then he sent a plague of frogs hop-hop-hopping into every nook and cranny. Next the very dust on the ground was turned into gnats, and after that came a swarm of flies—so many that the air turned black!

After this God sent a plague among the animals, sparing only those belonging to the Hebrews. The next plague struck the Egyptians with horrible boils.

But still Pharaoh wouldn't change his mind!

69

Hail and Fire
(Exodus 9-10)

Next came thunder and heavy hail that stripped the land. The lightning struck again and again, and fires blazed! When this wasn't enough to persuade Pharaoh, the plants that survived the storms were eaten by a swarm of locusts. Nothing green remained in all of Egypt. After this God sent total darkness for three whole days.

Each time Pharaoh pretended that he would relent, yet once the plague was lifted, he refused to let the Hebrews go. God hardened Pharaoh's heart to teach him a lesson, show his true power, and to make sure the story was told throughout the world.

But now the time had come for the most dreadful plague of all…

71

The Passover
(Exodus 11-12)

Moses warned Pharaoh that God would pass through the country at midnight, and every firstborn son in the land—from the son of Pharaoh himself to the son of the lowliest slave girl and even the firstborn of the animals—would die. Pharaoh would not listen!

Moses told his people that each family must kill a lamb, smear the blood on the door frame, and eat the meat in a special way.

On the next day, the land was filled with the sound of mourning because all the firstborn sons had died, even Pharaoh's son. But God had passed over the houses of the Israelites, and they were spared!

Now the Egyptians couldn't get rid of the Hebrews quick enough, and so Moses and his people prepared to leave Egypt.

73

No Way Out!
(Exodus 14)

The Hebrews traveled across the desert toward the Red Sea. By day God sent a column of cloud to guide them, and by night they followed a pillar of fire. Yet their troubles weren't over. Pharaoh was sorry he had let them go and had sent an army after them!

All those hooves and wheels set off a huge cloud of dust that the Hebrews could see from miles away. They panicked because their way of escape was barred by the waters of the Red Sea.

"Why did you bring us all this way just to have us killed or dragged back into slavery?" cried the terrified Hebrews to Moses. "It would have been better for us to serve the Egyptians than to die in the desert!"

Crossing the Red Sea
(Exodus 14)

The people grew more terrified as the army came nearer and nearer, but Moses did not give up his faith in God. "God will look after us," he said confidently, "and he will crush our enemy."

Then God told Moses to raise his staff and stretch out his hand over the sea to divide the water so that the Israelites could go through the sea on dry ground.

So Moses stood before the sea and raised his hand, and all that night the Lord drove the sea back with a strong wind and turned it into dry land. The waters were divided, and the Israelites went through the sea on dry ground with a wall of water on their right and on their left!

Drowned!
(Exodus 15)

The Egyptians were close on the heels of the Hebrews and swiftly followed them into the sea along the path that God had made. But God struck them with confusion so that the wheels of the chariots came off, and everywhere there was chaos. Then he closed the waters together, and the Egyptians were all swept under the sea! None of that mighty army survived—not one single horse, not one single soldier!

The people of Israel, safe on the far shore of the Red Sea, were filled with gratitude and relief and sang and danced with joy. They knew that their God was both mighty and merciful, and they praised him greatly.

Food and Water in the Desert
(Exodus 15-17)

Moses led his people into the hot, dry desert. They soon forgot what God had done for them and began to complain. "Either we shall die of thirst or of starvation!" they wailed. "Why did you bring us out of Egypt just to die here?"

Once again God helped his people. In the evenings quail would come into the camp, and in the mornings the ground would be covered with white flakes that tasted like wafers made with honey. They called it "manna." For all the time that they were in the desert, God provided quail, manna, and fresh drinking water that flowed from a rock, which God told Moses to hit with his staff.

The Ten Commandments
(Exodus 19-20)

Moses led the people to Mount Sinai. There God spoke to him and gave him special instructions to pass on to his people:

"You shall have no other gods before me.

"You shall not make false idols.

"You shall not misuse my name.

"Remember the Sabbath and keep it holy.

"Honor your father and mother.

"You shall not murder.

"You shall not commit adultery.

"You shall not steal.

"You shall not tell lies.

"You shall not envy anything that belongs to your neighbor."

Moses told the people what God had commanded, and they promised to obey.

83

The Golden Calf
(Exodus 32)

Moses was on the mountain for so long that the people thought he wasn't coming back. They asked Aaron to make them gods to lead them, so Aaron used their gold jewelry to make a golden calf, which he placed on an altar. The people began to worship it!

God was furious and would have destroyed all of them, but Moses begged him not to. Then Moses came down from the mountain with the commandments written on two stone tablets and saw the people singing and dancing around the golden calf. Moses was so angry that he threw the tablets to the ground where they shattered! Then he burned the calf and ground it into powder!

God punished those who had sinned with a dreadful plague.

85

The Twelve Spies
(Numbers 13-14)

After this the Ten Commandments were placed on two new tablets, and the people prepared a special place for them to be kept. Then it was time for them to travel to the land God had promised them.

At last they were close enough for Moses to send twelve men to explore Canaan, the Promised Land. They came back laden with juicy fruit. "The land really does flow with milk and honey," they said, "but it is far too well defended!" Only two of the men trusted in God enough to believe they could take the land he had promised them.

God was so angry with his people for not trusting him that he left them to wander in the desert for another forty years!

Water from the Rock
(Numbers 20)

Once again the people were grumbling. The desert was hot, and they were thirsty. Moses and Aaron asked for God's help, and he told them to take the staff and gather everyone in front of a large rock. "Speak to that rock before their eyes, and it will pour out its water," he commanded them.

This they did, but Moses also struck the stone twice with his staff. The water gushed out, and the grateful people rushed to fill their jugs with the cool water.

But God was disappointed that Moses hadn't followed his instructions or given him the credit, and so God told the brothers that they would never enter the Promised Land.

Moses Sees the Promised Land
(Deuteronomy 33-34)

When Moses was old, he asked God to choose someone to lead the people after his death. God chose Joshua, a good man.

It was time for Moses to leave his people. Before he went, he tried to tell them how blessed they were to have God on their side as their shield and their sword.

Then Moses climbed a mountain, and God showed him the land of Canaan in the distance. Moses died on the mountain. He was a hundred and twenty years old! The people were very sad. They knew there would never be another prophet like Moses, who had spoken with God face-to-face.

The Walls of Jericho
(Joshua 6)

For years the Israelites wandered in the desert, but now it was time for them to take the Promised Land. After God helped them across the River Jordan, they stood before the strong walls of Jericho. Joshua knew God would help them again.

God told Joshua exactly what to do. Once a day for six days, the Israelite army marched quietly around the city while priests blew on trumpets. On the seventh day, when the trumpets sounded, the people raised a mighty cry, and the city walls trembled and collapsed before them!

The soldiers charged in and took the city, and the story of how the Lord had helped Joshua take Jericho spread far and wide.

93

The Sun and Moon Stand Still
(Joshua 10)

After Joshua and his men marched all night to reach Gibeon to help some allies, they arrived and unexpectedly faced five Amorite kings and their armies.

But God was on Joshua's side. God sent great hailstones to fall on the enemy, and soon Joshua knew the Israelites were winning—but he also knew that night would fall before they could finish the battle.

Then Joshua called out, "Sun, stand still over Gibeon, and you, moon, over the Valley of Aijalon!" God listened to Joshua and made the sun and the moon stand still until Joshua and his men had won the battle!

The Israelites had many more battles to win, but with God's help, the land was finally theirs.

Gideon and the Three Hundred
(Judges 7)

Gideon was chosen by God to help his people defeat their enemies, the Midianites. Many men rallied with Gideon, but God told him that there were too many. First he had Gideon send home all those who were scared. Then he told Gideon to keep only those who cupped the water in their hands when they drank from the river. Only three hundred men remained!

That night Gideon and his men crept down to the enemy camp carrying trumpets and torches in jars. At a signal they all blew their trumpets, smashed the jars, and shouted loudly. The Midianites were so startled that they fled in terror, and in this way, Gideon and God won the battle with just three hundred men!

97

Faithful Ruth
(Ruth 1)

Naomi was moving back to Bethlehem. Her husband and sons had died, and she wanted to go home. She begged her beloved daughters-in-law, Orpah and Ruth, to stay behind because she was penniless and knew that her life would be hard.

Orpah and Ruth loved Naomi dearly and did not want to stay behind, but finally Orpah agreed to go home.

Loyal Ruth, however, said earnestly, "Don't ask me to leave! I will go wherever you go. Your people will be my people, and your God will be my God!"

Ruth's Reward
(Ruth 2-4)

So it was that Ruth and Naomi came to Bethlehem. Soon they had no food left, and brave Ruth went out into the fields, where workers were harvesting the crops, and asked the owner if she could pick up any of the barley that his workers left behind.

This man was Boaz, and he kindly let Ruth work in his fields. He told his servants to share their food with her. When Ruth returned with a full basket of food, Naomi knew that the Lord was looking after them because Boaz was a relation of hers.

In time Ruth married Boaz, and when they had a son, there was no happier woman in the whole of Bethlehem than Naomi!

Samson, the Strong
(Judges 13-14)

Samson was strong and brave—stronger and braver than any other man around!

When he was born, God told his parents that he was special and that one day he would deliver the Israelites from their enemies, the wicked Philistines. As a sign to show how special he was and that he belonged to God, Samson's parents never once cut his hair!

One day when Samson was grown up, he was pounced upon by one of the fierce lions that roamed the land of Canaan. Samson was filled with the Spirit of the Lord and became so strong that he was able to kill the beast with his bare hands!

Samson and Delilah
(Judges 16)

The Philistines came to hate and fear Samson for he carried out many attacks against them. So when he fell in love with Delilah, a beautiful Philistine woman, they bribed her to find out the secret of Samson's strength.

Night after night treacherous Delilah pleaded with Samson to tell her his secret. In the end he told her, "If anyone were to cut my hair off, then I would lose all my strength."

When Samson awoke, he discovered that the Philistines had come into his room and cut off his hair. Now he was powerless as they bound and blinded him and threw him into prison!

Retribution!
(Judges 16)

Over time Samson's hair grew back.

One day the Philistine leaders were all gathered for a feast in a crowded temple. Samson was brought out of the prison to be made fun of and chained between the two central pillars of the temple.

Then Samson prayed to God with all his heart, "Give me strength just one more time, Lord, so I can take revenge upon my enemies!"

Once more Samson was filled with strength. He pushed against the pillars with all his might. As they toppled, the temple crashed down, killing everyone inside! Samson killed more of his enemies with this final act than he had killed in all of his life.

David in the Army Camp

(1 Samuel 17)

David was just a shepherd boy and the youngest of his family. Even though his many brothers were older and stronger than he was, God chose him as the future leader of Israel!

The Israelites were at war with the Philistines, and the two armies had gathered to do battle when David brought food to his brothers who were fighting in the army.

The Philistines had a mighty champion. His name was Goliath, and he was powerful and strong—and ten feet tall! Goliath challenged the Israelites to single combat, but no one dared to fight him. No one, that is, apart from David!

109

A Stone in a Sling
(1 Samuel 17)

Young David stood before Goliath. No one else had dared to fight this terrible warrior! God had been with David when he had protected his sheep from lions and bears, and David knew that God would be with him now. He stood there with nothing but his staff, a sling, and five stones.

Goliath laughed at the boy, but David fearlessly ran forward, putting a stone in his sling and flinging it with all his might. It hit Goliath on his forehead. When Goliath fell to the ground, David raced up and cut off the giant's head with Goliath's own sword!

The Philistines were so shocked that they turned and ran away!

The Lord Is My Shepherd
(Psalm 23)

David went on to become a good king. He wrote many special prayers or songs to God. They are known as psalms.

The Lord is my shepherd;
  he will make sure I have everything I need.
He lets me rest in green meadows;
  he leads me beside quiet streams to drink.
He refreshes my soul.
He shows me the right way to go
  so that I can bring honor to his name.

Even though I walk through the darkest of valleys,
  I will fear nothing, for you are with me;
  your rod and shepherd's crook make me feel safe.

You prepare a feast for me in front of my enemies
  and honor me as your guest.
You give me so much more than I need.
Your kindness and love will be with me
  every day of my life,
  and I will live forever in your house, Lord.

Psalm 23

How Wonderful Is Your Name!

(Psalm 8)

Oh Lord, how wonderful is your name!
When I think about how you made
   the heavens,
     and how you placed the moon and stars
     in the sky,
     I wonder how you can care about
     human beings.
We are so small!

Yet you have made us only a little lower
   than the angels.
You have made us rulers over everything
   you created:
     the birds and the beasts,
     the fish in the sea.
We rule over all of them!

Oh Lord, how wonderful is your name!

Psalm 8

God Is My Fortress
(Psalm 18)

How I love you, Lord!
You are my fortress and my rescuer;
  I am always safe with you.
You are like a shield.
When I was scared and in danger,
  I called out for help, and you rescued me
  from my enemies.
When I cried out to you, you heard me;
  you reached down from the heavens
  and pulled me out of deep waters.

Oh Lord, you keep my lamp burning,
  and you turn my darkness into light.
With your help I can do anything.
I can face my enemies, and
  I can climb high walls.
You made me strong and kept me safe; you
  hold me up; you make a wide path for
  my feet, so I can stand strong and secure.
Because of you I am safe.
Oh Lord, I will praise your name
  wherever I go!

Psalm 18

Do Not Be Far from Me
(Psalm 22)

Lord, I feel so alone and miserable.
Everyone makes fun of me.
I am surrounded by trouble,
*   and there is no one to help me.*
My enemies are waiting to pounce
*   like a pack of wild dogs.*
So do not stay away, my Lord.
Come quickly to help me.
Rescue me from these wild beasts!

I will tell everyone what you have done.
I will praise your name to everyone I meet,
*   for you don't neglect those who are in trouble;*
*   you don't turn away from them,*
*   but answer when they call for help.*
Everyone will know that you saved your people.

Psalm 22

On Good Friday, Christians remember how
Jesus died. Many of them read or sing Psalm 22
and believe that it is not only about the suffering
of King David, but that it is also about the
suffering of Jesus.

119

Water in the Desert
(Psalm 63)

You, God, are my God!
I seek you with all my heart.
I need you
*   like a dry desert needs water.*

I have seen how wonderful you are.
Your love is better than life itself;
*   it will satisfy me like the richest food.*

When I lie in my bed, I will remember
*   you and think of you all night long.*

You have always been there to help me.
Your wings protect me,
*   and when I cling to you,*
*   your hand keeps me safe.*

Psalm 63

King David wrote this psalm when he
was in the desert of Judah.

God Speaks to Solomon
(1 Kings 3)

Solomon was David's son. When David died as an old man, Solomon was crowned king. Soon after, God spoke to Solomon in a dream and told him he would give him whatever he asked for.

Solomon thought carefully, and then instead of asking for wealth or long life or great victories, he asked for wisdom to rule wisely over God's people for he wanted to be a good king like his father.

God was pleased with Solomon's answer. "I will give you wisdom," God said, "but I will also give you those things you didn't ask for!"

When Solomon awoke, he felt comforted and strengthened knowing that God was with him.

123

A Wise Ruler
(1 Kings 3)

Two women came before Solomon. They held a baby between them. They had both had babies at the same time, and one of the babies had died. Now they both said that this baby was theirs!

The king called for a sword and then told a guard, "Cut the child in two and give half to one woman and half to the other."

One woman cried out in horror, "No! No, my lord! Give her the baby! Don't kill him! I would rather she look after him than he die!" The other woman nodded for she thought this was fair.

Then Solomon said, "Give the baby to the first woman. Do not kill him; she is his true mother."

Then people realized how wise and clever God had made Solomon.

125

The Widow and the Prophet
(1 Kings 17)

There was a dreadful drought all across the land. God sent his prophet Elijah to Sidon, and when he reached the city gates, he met a woman gathering firewood and asked for a drink of water. The kind widow went to fetch him some, even though water was scarce. As she was going, Elijah asked for some bread.

"I'm afraid I have no bread," she replied. "I have only a handful of flour and a little olive oil in a jug. I am gathering a few sticks to take home and make one last meal for myself and my son."

127

The Amazing Jar of Oil
(1 Kings 17)

Elijah told the widow not to worry but to go home and make a small loaf of bread for him first and then one for herself and her son. He said that God had promised that her flour and oil would not run out until the day that rain fell on the land.

The kind widow did as Elijah had asked and found that when she had made one loaf, she still had enough flour and oil to make another. And so it went on day after day. There was always enough food for Elijah and for the widow and her young son.

Jonah Disobeys God
(Jonah 1)

Jonah was a prophet. One day God told him to go to Nineveh, which was many miles away, and tell the people that unless they turned from their wicked ways, God would destroy their fine city.

Now, the people of Nineveh were enemies of the Jews, and Jonah did not want to warn them so that God could spare them. He thought they deserved to be punished!

So instead of doing as God had told him, Jonah boarded a ship heading in the opposite direction from Nineveh. He was trying to run away from God—but, of course, God is everywhere!

The Dreadful Storm
(Jonah 1)

A dreadful storm sprang up from nowhere. The winds howled, and the waves towered above the ship. The terrified sailors drew straws to see who had angered the gods. When Jonah picked the short straw, they asked him what he had done, and Jonah told them that he was running away from his God. As he spoke he realized how foolish and wicked he had been. He told them that they must cast him over the side for God was angry with only him.

The sea became very rough when the sailors reluctantly lowered Jonah over the side. Then instantly the sea became calm! The amazed sailors now realized that God was the one true God and began to pray to him with all their hearts.

133

The Big Fish
(Jonah 2)

What about Jonah? He sank swiftly to the bottom of the sea, certain he was going to die. But before he could take his last breath, God sent an enormous fish to swallow Jonah whole, and there inside the fish, Jonah could breathe once again and was safe.

For three days and nights, Jonah sat inside the belly of the fish. He had plenty of time to feel very sorry for having disobeyed God, and so he prayed. Jonah thanked God for saving him and let him know how sorry he was.

Then God commanded the fish to spit Jonah up, safe and sound and onto dry land. When God once again asked him to take his message to Nineveh, Jonah was ready to do as he was told!

Hezekiah's Prayer
(2 Kings 18-20, 2 Chron. 29-32)

When King Hezekiah was on the throne of Judah, the mighty army of Assyria marched on Jerusalem and demanded that it surrender. "Your God won't be able to save you!" the enemy soldiers jeered.

The people cowered in fear, but Hezekiah prayed to God. "You are the only true God," he said. "I place all my trust in you. Save us from these Assyrians who insult you so that all may know that you alone, Lord, are God."

When the sun came up the next morning, it rose on the dead bodies of thousands and thousands of Assyrian soldiers. After that the Assyrians who were still alive packed up their things and marched home as quickly as they could!

137

A Fiery Furnace
(Daniel 3)

Shadrach, Meshach, and Abednego, exiles from Jerusalem, had been bound and thrown into a furnace by King Nebuchadnezzar for refusing to bow down before a gold statue and saying that they would never bow down to anyone but their God. The furnace was so hot that the guards were scorched to death!

Nebuchadnezzar suddenly leaped up in disbelief because within the furnace he could see the men walking freely, and with them was one who looked like the Son of God!

The king called to them to come out, and the friends walked from the flames quite unharmed.

Nebuchadnezzar was amazed and announced that their God was truly to be praised for saving his loyal servants in this way.

139

The Sneaky Trap
(Daniel 6)

Daniel had an important job in the court of King Darius of Persia. He was an exile from Jerusalem, but the king trusted him. The other officials were jealous. Knowing that Daniel prayed every day, they came up with a plan.

They had the king sign an order stating that for thirty days anyone asking anything of any god or man except the king should be thrown into a den of lions!

Daniel prayed just as he had always done. He would not stop or even hide what he was doing. His enemies rushed to the king and told him. King Darius was sad, but he could not change the law.

"You have been loyal to your God. I hope he can save you," he said sadly as Daniel was thrown to the lions!

141

In the Lions' Den
(Daniel 6)

That evening the king did not sleep a wink. At first light he rushed down to the pit. "Daniel!" he cried out, more in desperation than hope. "Has your God been able to save you?"

How thrilled and amazed he was when he saw Daniel completely unharmed and sitting with the lions. God had sent an angel to shut the mouths of the lions!

"Your God truly is wonderful!" said King Darius, and he ordered that from then on, everyone in the kingdom should respect and honor Daniel's God.

As for the wicked men who had tricked the king, they were thrown into the pit— and this time the lions were ruthless!

Beautiful Esther
(Esther 2)

King Xerxes of Persia had sent his queen away because he was angry with her. Now he needed a new queen, and so servants were sent out to find all the beautiful young maidens of the land and bring them to the palace.

Among them was a lovely young girl named Esther, and as soon as King Xerxes saw her, he declared that she would be his wife. Esther did not tell him she was a Jew.

Her cousin Mordecai was given a position in the king's court and chanced to overhear a plot against the king's life. When Esther told the king, the treacherous guards were hanged. All this was written down in the official records, but the king forgot to reward the man who had saved his life!

145

A Dreadful Enemy
(Esther 3-4)

Unfortunately, Mordecai soon made a dreadful enemy in court. Haman, the king's prime minister, thought very well of himself and was offended when Mordecai refused to bow to him.

When Haman found out that Mordecai was a Jew, he tricked the king into signing a decree that ordered the killing of all Jews in the empire!

When Mordecai learned of it, he sent a message to Esther, begging her to plead their case before the king.

The Brave Queen
(Esther 4-5)

Esther was terrified. To go before the king without a summons was punishable by death. Only if the king held out his scepter would the person be spared. Mordecai sent another message to Esther saying, "You must help the Jews or God will be angry. Maybe he made you queen precisely so that you could save his people."

Esther was scared but made up her mind to go to the king.

When he saw Esther, he smiled, held out his golden scepter, and said, "Tell me what you want and you shall have it— even if it is half my empire!"

Esther could not bring herself to ask the king there and then. Instead, she invited him and Haman to a banquet in her rooms.

149

The Banquet
(Esther 5,6,7)

By the time Haman arrived at the queen's banquet, he was in a very bad mood. Angry with Mordecai for still refusing to bow, he had arranged to have a gallows built and was going to ask the king to hang Mordecai when, in a strange twist of events, the king realized that Mordecai was the one who had saved his life. He then ordered the Jew to be honored.

Things would only get worse! When Queen Esther finally plucked up courage to tell her husband about the decree to kill the Jews, the king was so furious with his prime minister that he sentenced Haman to be hung on the very gallows Haman had built!

151

Esther Saves the Day
(Esther 8-9)

Haman was dead, but the danger was not over. A decree stamped with the royal seal couldn't be changed. The Jews were still sentenced to death. Brave Esther begged the king again for help.

The king had Mordecai send another proclamation across the empire stating that all Jews may arm themselves and fight back if they are attacked.

So when the followers of Haman tried to massacre the Jewish people, the Jews fought back and destroyed them utterly! The Jews were saved! Ever since then the Jews have celebrated the holy festival of Purim each year in gratitude for God's deliverance through Esther and Mordecai.

Mary Is Chosen by God
(Luke 1)

Mary lived in Galilee in a town called Nazareth. She was engaged to a carpenter named Joseph. One day an angel appeared before her.

"Do not be afraid," he told the startled girl. "God has chosen you for a very special honor. You will give birth to a son, and you are to call him Jesus. He will be God's own Son, and his kingdom will never end!"

Mary was filled with wonder. "How can this be?" she asked softly. "I am not even married."

"Everything is possible for God," replied the angel.

Mary bowed her head humbly and said, "It will be as God wills it."

155

God Speaks to Joseph
(Matthew 1)

When Joseph found out that Mary was going to have a baby, he thought she had been unfaithful to him and was very upset. He decided to break off the marriage, but before he could do anything, God spoke to him in a dream.

"Mary has not been unfaithful. The baby she is carrying was conceived by the Holy Spirit. She will give birth to a son, and you will call him Jesus. He will save his people from their sins."

When Joseph awoke, he felt so much happier. Mary had been true to him, and now he would do all he could to keep her and the child safe. They were married without delay!

Traveling to Bethlehem
(Luke 1-2)

Around this time the emperor of Rome ordered a census of all the people he ruled over. He wanted to make sure that everyone paid their taxes. All the people throughout the land ruled by Rome had to go to their hometown to be counted.

Joseph's family was descended from King David, and so he and Mary had to travel to Bethlehem where King David had been born. Mary's baby was due to be born any day, and the journey was long and hard, but they had to do as the emperor ordered.

No Room at the Inn
(Luke 2)

When Mary and Joseph finally arrived in Bethlehem, they were tired and desperately wanted to find a room for the night because the time had come for Mary's baby to be born.

But the town was filled to bursting. Everyone had come to be counted. Every single inn was full, and there was nowhere for them to stay!

Born in a Manger
(Luke 2)

At last an innkeeper said to them, "I have no rooms available, but there is somewhere you can spend the night." He showed them to a stable where the animals were kept. It was dirty and smelly, but it was the best he could do.

That night Mary's baby was born. She wrapped him in strips of cloth and then laid him gently on clean straw in a manger. Mary and Joseph looked down upon their son with joy, and they named him Jesus just as the angel had told them to.

The Shepherds on the Hillside
(Luke 2)

That same night some shepherds were keeping watch over their flocks in the hills above Bethlehem. Suddenly the sky was filled with a blinding light!

As they fell to the ground in fear, an angel spoke to them. "Do not be afraid. I bring you good news. Today in the town of David, a Savior has been born to you; he is the Messiah, the Lord. Go and see for yourselves. You will find him wrapped in cloths and lying in a manger."

Then the whole sky was filled with angels praising God!

The Baby King
(Luke 2)

When the angels left, the shepherds looked at one another in amazement. Although they could hardly believe what had just happened, they all knew one thing—they simply had to go to Bethlehem to see this baby for themselves.

The shepherds made sure that the sheep were safe and then hurried down to Bethlehem as fast as they could. They made their way to the stable, and there they found the baby lying in the manger just as they had been told. Filled with wonder and awe, the shepherds fell to their knees before the tiny baby boy who would change the world forever.

Then they rushed off to tell everyone the wonderful news!

167

Following a Star
(Matthew 2)

In a distant land, three wise men had been studying the stars. When they found a really bright star shining in the skies, they followed it all the way to Judea because they believed it was a sign that a great king had been born.

They asked King Herod in Jerusalem if he could show them the way to the baby who would be the King of the Jews. Herod was horrified! He didn't want another king around. His advisors told him of a prophecy that the new king would be born in the city of King David—in Bethlehem.

The cunning king sent the wise men to Bethlehem, saying, "Once you have found him, come back and tell me where he is so that I can visit him too!"

Gifts for a King
(Matthew 2)

The wise men followed the star to Bethlehem where they found baby Jesus in a humble house.

There they knelt before him and presented him with fine gifts of gold, sweet-smelling frankincense, and a spicy ointment called myrrh.

Then they left to begin their long journey home—but they did not stop off at Herod's palace because God had warned them in a dream not to tell Herod where the baby was.

Escape to Egypt
(Matthew 2)

Herod was furious when he realized the wise men weren't coming back. Determined there should be no other king, he gave an order that all boys under the age of two should be killed!

Just after the wise men left Bethlehem, an angel appeared to Joseph in a dream, warning him to flee to Egypt that very night. Joseph and Mary swiftly gathered their belongings, lifted baby Jesus gently from his bed, and set off in haste on the long journey to Egypt.

They lived in Egypt until wicked King Herod died, and then they returned home to Nazareth. As the years passed, Jesus grew to be filled with grace and wisdom. God loved him, and so did everyone who knew him.

173

Water into Wine
(John 2)

When Jesus was grown up, he and some of his friends were invited to a wedding. Everyone was having a wonderful time—until the wine ran out! Jesus' mother, Mary, came to tell him about the problem. She hoped he would help.

Several huge, empty water jars stood nearby. Jesus told the servants to fill them with water, then pour the water into jugs, and take the jugs to the headwaiter. When the headwaiter took a taste, he was astonished. He exclaimed to the bridegroom, "You have saved the best wine until last!" The jugs were filled with delicious wine!

This was the first of many miracles that Jesus would perform.

You Can Make Me Clean
(Mark 1)

One day a man with a dreadful skin disease came up to Jesus and fell to his knees on the ground before him. "Sir, if you want to, you can make me clean," he begged humbly.

Filled with compassion, Jesus reached out to touch the man.

"I do want to," Jesus said kindly. "Be clean!" Immediately the man's skin was perfectly smooth and healthy!

The grateful man simply couldn't keep the wonderful news to himself, and before long so many people wanted to come and see Jesus that he could no longer go anywhere without being surrounded by crowds.

177

Where There's a Will
(Mark 2)

Everyone was excited because Jesus was in town. Four men especially wanted to see him. Their friend was paralyzed and couldn't walk. Jesus could heal him!

But the house was so packed that they couldn't get close. Still they didn't give up. They made a hole in the roof and lowered the man down through it on a mat!

Jesus saw how strongly they believed in him and said to the man, "Your sins are forgiven," for forgiveness was the most important thing of all.

Then he said, "Get up, pick up your mat, and go home." The man stood up, picked up the mat, and walked out, and everyone was amazed!

179

Just Say the Word
(Matthew 8)

Once a Roman officer came to ask Jesus for his help because one of his servants was very ill. Jesus asked, "Shall I come and heal him?"

The officer replied, "Lord, I don't deserve that. But if you just say the word, I know that my servant will be healed in the same way that when I order my soldiers to do something, they do it." The officer believed in Jesus so completely that he did not even need him to visit his servant!

Jesus said to the crowd, "I tell you, I have never found faith like this before, not even in Israel!"

And when the officer returned to his house, sure enough, he found his servant up on his feet and feeling perfectly well again!

181

The Widow's Son
(Luke 7)

One day when Jesus and his disciples were entering a town, they arrived in time to see a funeral procession coming out through the city gates. The dead man was the only son of a widow, and she was heartbroken.

When Jesus saw her, his heart was filled with pity. He walked up to her and said gently, "Don't cry." Then he moved over and touched the stretcher, and the men carrying it stopped.

Jesus said, "Young man, get up!"

At his words, to the astonishment and awe of the mourners, the dead man sat up and began to talk! Jesus led him to his mother, who was filled with thankfulness and joy.

183

Just a Touch
(Luke 8)

Jairus was desperate. His little girl was dreadfully ill, and he was worried that Jesus wouldn't be able to make his way through the crowds and to his home in time. Suddenly, Jesus stopped still and asked who had touched him. "Master, everyone is touching you!" said a disciple, but Jesus knew that he had been touched in a special way.

As he looked around, a woman stepped forward. "Lord, it was me," she said nervously. For years she had been ill and nobody had been able to help her, but she knew that if she could just get close to Jesus, she would be healed. Sure enough, the moment she had managed to touch his cloak, she was well!

Jesus turned to her and said, "Your faith has healed you. Go home."

Just Sleeping
(Mark 5)

Passing through the crowds and speaking to the woman had taken up precious time. Just then a messenger ran up to say that Jairus' daughter was dead! Poor Jairus was heartbroken, but Jesus kept on walking. "Trust me, Jairus," he said.

They arrived at the house to the sound of weeping. "Why are you carrying on so?" Jesus asked. "The girl is not dead. She is just sleeping." Then he went to her room, took one of her hands in his own, and whispered, "Wake up, my child."

In that instant the child opened her eyes. She smiled at Jesus and hugged her overjoyed parents!

187

The Amazing Meal
(Mark 6)

A huge crowd had gathered to listen to Jesus, and by evening everyone was very hungry. Jesus told his disciples to give the people something to eat. "But, Master," they replied, "there are thousands of people, and we only have five loaves of bread and two fish!"

Jesus took the loaves and the fish, looked up to heaven, and broke them into pieces. He gave the food to the disciples, who took it to the people and then came back for more. He filled up the baskets again…and again…and again! There were still bread and fish left in the baskets when they fed the very last of the people! More than five thousand people were fed that day—with five loaves of bread and two fish!

189

Calming the Storm
(Matthew 8)

As Jesus and his disciples were sailing across the lake, Jesus fell asleep. Suddenly, the skies darkened, rain poured down, and a fierce storm struck! Huge waves tossed the boat, and the disciples were terrified of capsizing.

Jesus lay sleeping. The frightened disciples woke him and begged him to save them. Jesus looked up at them and said, "Why are you afraid? You have so little faith!"

Then he stood up calmly and spread his arms wide. Facing into the wind and rain, he commanded, "Be still!" At once the wind and waves died down and all was calm!

The disciples were amazed. "Even the wind and waves obey him!" they said in awe.

Walking on Water
(Matthew 14)

It was night and the waves tossed the boat violently. Jesus had gone ashore to pray, and the disciples were afraid. When they saw a figure walking toward them on the water, they became even more scared until they heard Jesus calmly say, "It is I. Do not be afraid."

"Lord," said Simon Peter, "if it is you, tell me to come to you." When Jesus did so, Peter put first one foot and then the other gingerly in the water and bravely stood up—on the water! But when he looked at the waves, his courage failed him, and he began to sink!

Jesus took his hand, and together they walked to the boat. The wind died down and the water became calm. "Truly you are the Son of God," said the disciples.

Lazarus Lives!
(John 11)

Jesus received a message from his friends Martha and Mary, telling him that their brother Lazarus was very ill. But by the time Jesus arrived, Lazarus was dead!

Jesus comforted Martha by saying, "He will rise again. Everyone who believes in me will live again, even though he has died."

But when Mary started crying too, Jesus wept and asked to be taken to the cave where Lazarus had been laid. When he arrived he told the men to roll away the stone, even though Lazarus had been dead for four days.

Jesus prayed and gave thanks to God. Then he said loudly, "Lazarus, come out!"

Everyone watched in wonder as a figure wrapped with strips of linen emerged from the cave. It was Lazarus, and he was alive!

195

Blind Bartimaeus
(Luke 18)

Blind Bartimaeus was begging by the roadside and heard a great commotion. When he learned that it was Jesus of Nazareth, he struggled to his feet and called out, "Jesus, Son of David, have mercy on me!"

People shushed him, but he kept calling. Jesus stopped by the roadside and asked the blind man, "What do you want me to do for you?"

Bartimaeus fell to his knees. "Lord, I want to see!" he begged.

"Receive your sight," said Jesus. "Your faith has healed you." Immediately Bartimaeus' eyes were cleared, and he could see everything! He praised God with all his heart. When all the people saw, they praised God too!

The Sower
(Matthew 13)

Many of the people who came to listen to Jesus were uneducated. They worked on the land or were craftsmen. Jesus tried to pass on his message in a way that they would understand.

His stories, often called parables, let people think things through for themselves. To some they would just be stories, but others would understand the real message…

Once Jesus told his followers a story about a farmer who sowed some seeds. The seeds all fell in different places. Some fell on the path and were trampled on or eaten by birds. Some fell on rocky ground where they withered because their roots could not reach the soil. Some fell among weeds that choked them. Only those few that fell on good soil grew into strong, healthy plants.

Jesus said that he is like the farmer and the seeds are like the message he brought from God. The seeds that fell on the path and were eaten by birds are like those people who hear the good news but pay no attention. Those on rocky ground are like people who believe for a while, but when life gets difficult, they give up easily—their faith doesn't have strong roots. The seeds that fell among weeds are like those who hear but let themselves become distracted and choked by other things.

But the seeds that fell on good soil are like those people who hear God's message and hold it in their heart. Their faith grows and grows!

The Weeds
(Matthew 13)

Jesus told another parable.

"Once a farmer sowed good seed in his field, but that night his enemy sowed weeds among the wheat. When the wheat began to grow, weeds grew too.

"His servants asked if they should pull them up, but the owner said, 'If you pull the weeds up, you may pull some of the wheat up too. We must let both grow until harvest, and then we will burn the weeds and gather the wheat.'"

Jesus was talking about the end of time when everything that causes sin and all those people who do bad things will be weeded out of God's kingdom and destroyed. But the good people will be saved and will enter the kingdom of their Father!

The Lost Son
(Luke 15)

Jesus told a story to explain how happy God was when sinners returned to him.

"There was once a man with two sons. The younger one asked for his share of the property so he could go out into the world. He soon spent it all on enjoying himself. He ended up working for a farmer and was so hungry that sometimes he wished he could eat the food he was giving to the pigs!

"At last he came to his senses and set off for home to tell his father how sorry he was. *I'm not worthy to be his son, but maybe he will let me work on the farm,* he hoped.

"When his father saw his young son coming, he rushed out and threw his arms around him. The young man tried to tell his father that he was not fit to be called his son, but his father told the servants to bring his finest robe for him to wear and to kill the prize calf for a feast.

"The older son was outraged! He had worked hard for his father all this time, and nobody had ever held a feast for him. Yet here came his brother, having squandered all his money, and his father couldn't wait to kill the calf and welcome him home!

"'My son,' the father said, 'you are always with me, and all I have is yours. Celebrate with me now, for your brother was dead to me and is alive again. He was lost and is found!'"

The Good Samaritan
(Luke 10)

Once someone asked Jesus what the Law meant when it said we must love our neighbors as much as ourselves. "Who is my neighbor?" he asked. Jesus told him this story.

"A man was going from Jerusalem to Jericho when he was attacked by robbers who stole everything before leaving him by the roadside half dead.

"Soon a priest passed by. When he saw the man, he crossed to the other side of the road and continued on his way. Then a Levite came along. He also hurried on his way without stopping.

"Nobody wanted to get involved. They were all too busy or too important or too scared to help!

209

"Now, the next person to come along was a Samaritan. The Samaritans are not friends of the Jews, but when this traveler saw the man lying by the roadside, his heart was filled with pity.

"The Samaritan carefully washed and bandaged the man's wounds, took him on his donkey to an inn, and gave the innkeeper money to look after the man until he was well."

Jesus looked at the man who had posed the question and asked who he thought had been a good neighbor to the injured man.

The man sheepishly replied, "The one who was kind to him."

Then Jesus told him, "Then go and be like him."

211

The Last Will Be First
(Matthew 20)

"The kingdom of heaven," said Jesus to his followers, "is like the vineyard owner who hired workers—some early in the morning, some at lunchtime, and some in the afternoon. When evening came, the owner told his foreman to pay the workers, beginning with the last ones hired, and to give them all the same amount of money he had promised to those hired first.

"The first workers were angry because they had worked longer. The owner answered, 'Didn't you agree to work for this amount? I want to give the one hired last the same as you. Are you annoyed because I am generous?'

"So the last will be first, and the first will be last."

213

The Two Builders
(Luke 6)

Jesus told the crowds who came to hear him, "If you listen to my teaching and follow it, then you are wise and like the person who builds his house on solid rock. Even if the rain pours down, the rivers flood, and the winds rage, the house won't collapse. It is built on solid rock!

"But he who listens and doesn't obey is foolish and like a person who builds a house on sand without any foundations.

"The house is quickly built, but when the rains and floods and winds come, the house will not be able to stand against them. It will collapse and be utterly destroyed!"

Jesus Enters Jerusalem
(John 12)

The city of Jerusalem was packed with people who had come to celebrate the Passover festival. It was also time for Jesus to start the last stage of his life on earth.

Jesus entered Jerusalem riding on a humble donkey. As his followers threw their cloaks or large palm leaves on the dusty ground before him, he was met by an enormous crowd because many had heard of the miracles he had performed. The religious leaders might have feared and hated Jesus, but many of the people truly saw him as their king, and they tried to give him a king's welcome.

But Jesus was sad because he knew that soon these people cheering him would turn against him.

217

Betrayal
(Matthew 26)

Jesus knew that his enemies were waiting for an opportunity to arrest him, but in the end it was one of his closest friends who betrayed him.

Judas Iscariot, one of the disciples, was greedy and dishonest. His greed made him do a very bad thing. Judas went to the chief priests in secret and asked them how much they would give him if he delivered Jesus into their hands.

The priests couldn't believe their ears! They knew that Judas was one of Jesus' closest friends. They offered him thirty pieces of silver—and Judas accepted!

From then on, Judas was simply waiting for the opportunity to hand Jesus over.

Like a Servant
(John 13)

It was nearly time for the Passover feast, and a kind man had set aside a room for the disciples to prepare for it. That night when they were eating, Jesus wrapped a towel around his waist, filled a basin with water, and while kneeling on the floor, began to wash and dry their feet like a servant.

All but one of the disciples were speechless. When Jesus knelt before Simon Peter, the disciple protested, "Lord, you mustn't wash my feet!"

Jesus replied gently, "You don't understand what I am doing, but later it will be clear to you."

Jesus had washed their feet like a servant so that they could learn to do the same for one another.

221

The Lord's Supper
(Matthew 26)

Jesus knew he would soon have to leave his friends. He was sad and troubled. "Soon one of you will betray me," he said. The disciples looked at one another in shock, but when Judas Iscariot left the room soon after, they didn't realize that he was the traitor.

Jesus passed around bread to represent his body and wine to represent his blood before telling them he would soon leave them.

Simon Peter cried out, "But, Lord, why can't I follow you? I would gladly lay down my life for you!"

"Would you, my friend?" asked Jesus gently. "And yet you will disown me three times before the cock crows." Peter was horrified. That could never happen!

A Night of Prayer
(Matthew 26)

Jesus and the disciples left the city to go to a quiet garden. Jesus prayed to his Father to look after his disciples and all those who would come to believe in him.

That night Jesus was deeply troubled because he knew what a dreadful time lay ahead. Even his dearest friends were no comfort to him. They kept falling asleep each time he went off to talk to his Father. Jesus felt very sad and very lonely.

When he woke his friends for the final time, he said, "The hour has come. You need to get up because the one who has betrayed me is here."

Betrayed with a Kiss
(Luke 22)

A crowd of armed people burst into the garden. At the head of them was Judas Iscariot. He had told the priests that he would kiss Jesus so that they would know whom to arrest. As Judas approached Jesus, Jesus said sadly, "Oh, Judas, would you betray the Son of Man with a kiss?"

Jesus then allowed the soldiers to arrest him. Peter struck out with his sword, but Jesus stopped him. "I am the one you have come to find," he told the crowd. "Let these others go. You had no need to come here with swords and clubs."

When the disciples realized that Jesus was going to allow himself to be taken prisoner, they fled in fear and despair.

The Cock Crows
(Mark 14)

Simon Peter followed the soldiers to a courtyard where he waited along with the guards who were warming themselves at the fire. One of the servants saw him and said, "Weren't you with Jesus?"

"No, you've got the wrong man," Peter whispered, fearful of what might happen if the soldiers heard.

The girl shrugged but said to one of the guards, "Don't you think he looks like one of Jesus' followers?"

"I told you I don't have anything to do with him!" Peter replied, panicking.

"You must be one of them," said one of the guards. "I can tell from your accent that you're from Galilee."

"I swear I've never met him!" cried Peter just as a cock crowed. Then Peter remembered what Jesus had said and wept in dismay.

229

Pilate Washes His Hands
(Matthew 27)

The priests and Pharisees wanted the Roman governor, Pontius Pilate, to order Jesus' execution. Pilate was unhappy because he knew Jesus was innocent.

There was one way out. During Passover it was the custom to release one prisoner. But when Pilate asked the crowd who to free, they called for the release of a criminal named Barabbas because the priests had stirred them up. When he asked what he should do with the king of the Jews, they roared, "Crucify him!"

Pilate did not want to order the execution—but neither did he want a riot! He sent for a bowl of water and washed his hands in it to show that he took no responsibility for Jesus' death.

231

Mocked
(Matthew 27)

Jesus was taken away. "Since you are the king of the Jews, let's dress you for the occasion!" the soldiers mocked, and they dressed him in a royal purple robe and put a crown of thorny branches on his head. Then they beat him and spat in his face before putting him back in his own clothes and leading him through the streets of the city.

They made him carry the wooden cross on his back. It was large and heavy, and Jesus had been dreadfully beaten. When he could do it no longer, they snatched someone from out of the crowd to carry it for him.

And so the dreadful procession made its way out of the city to the hill of Golgotha.

The Crucifixion
(Luke 23)

Soldiers nailed Jesus' hands and feet to the cross and put up a sign reading:

JESUS OF NAZARETH
KING OF THE JEWS

As they raised the cross, Jesus cried out, "Father, forgive them. They don't know what they are doing."

Two thieves were crucified beside Jesus. The first sneered at him, but the other said, "Be quiet! We deserve our punishment, but this man has done nothing wrong." Then he turned to Jesus and said, "Please remember me when you come into your kingdom." Jesus promised he would be with him that day in paradise.

The priests and Pharisees taunted him by saying, "If you come down from the cross now, we'll believe in you!"

235

It Is Finished!
(John 19)

At midday a shadow passed across the sun and darkness fell. At three o'clock in the afternoon, Jesus cried out in a loud voice, "My God, why have you forsaken me?" Then he called out, "It is finished!" With these words, he gave up his spirit.

When the Roman soldiers felt the ground move beneath their feet and saw how Jesus passed away, they were deeply shaken. "Surely he was the Son of God!" whispered one in amazement.

Because the next day was to be a special Sabbath, Jesus' body was taken down, wrapped in linen, and carried to a tomb. A large stone was rolled in front of the entrance, and soldiers were sent the following day to guard it.

237

The Empty Tomb
(Matthew 28)

Early on the first day of the week, before the sun had risen, Mary Magdalene and some other women went to anoint Jesus' body. As they came near the tomb, the earth shook, the guards were thrown to the ground, and the women saw that the stone had been rolled away. Inside the tomb, shining brighter than the sun, was an angel!

The terrified women fell to their knees as the angel said, "Why are you looking for the living among the dead? He is not here—he has risen! Didn't he tell you this would happen? Look and see. Then go and tell his disciples."

So the women, afraid yet filled with joy, hurried away to tell the disciples the news.

Alive!
(John 20)

Mary Magdalene stood outside the tomb. Two of the disciples had come, had seen the strips of linen, and had left in wonder and confusion. Now she was alone.

Just then she heard footsteps, and a man asked, "Why are you crying? Who are you looking for?"

Thinking this must be the gardener, she begged, "Sir, if you have moved him, please tell me where he is, and I will get him."

Although the man spoke only her name, Mary recognized that clear, gentle voice! She gasped and reached out, but Jesus said, "Do not hold on to me because I have not yet ascended to my Father. Go and tell the others!"

So Mary rushed off with the amazing news!

241

Thomas Doubts
(John 20)

That same evening, Jesus appeared to the disciples. At first they couldn't believe it and thought he might be a ghost, but he spoke to them and reassured them.

Thomas was not there, and when they told him about it, he couldn't believe them. He said, "Unless I put my finger where the nails were and touch the wound in his side, I will not believe."

A week later Jesus was with the disciples again. Turning to Thomas he said, "Put your finger in the wounds in my hands. Reach out and feel my side. Stop doubting and believe!" Thomas was overcome with joy!

Jesus said, "You only believed because you saw me yourself. Blessed are those people who believe without even seeing!"

243

The Ascension
(Acts 1)

Jesus and his friends were on a hillside outside Jerusalem. The time had come for Jesus to leave.

Jesus turned to his disciples. "You must stay here and wait for the gift that my Father has promised you. Soon you will be baptized with the Holy Spirit. Then you must spread my message not only in Jerusalem, but in every country throughout the world."

Then before their eyes, Jesus was taken up to heaven, and a cloud hid him from sight.

As they looked upward in wonder, two men dressed in white appeared beside them. "Why are you looking at the sky?" they asked. "Jesus has gone to be with God, but one day he will return!"

Let us be ready for that day!

245

Receiving the Holy Spirit
(Acts 2)

Ten days after Jesus was taken up to heaven, the disciples were meeting together when suddenly the house was filled with the sound of a mighty wind coming from heaven.

As they watched in wonder, tongues of fire seemed to rest on each person there! They were all filled with the Holy Spirit and began to speak in different languages —ones they had never spoken before!

Hearing the noise, a huge crowd gathered outside. They were amazed when the men came out and began telling them all about Jesus in many different languages!

After this the disciples became known as apostles for Jesus had sent them out to spread the good news to the world.

247

Peter Heals a Lame Man
(Acts 3-4)

A man sat begging outside the temple gates. He was lame and spent every day there, hoping for a spare coin or two. As the apostles Peter and John passed by, he looked up hopefully.

Peter stopped. "I don't have any money," he said, "but I can give you something far better!"

The lame man looked puzzled so Peter continued, "In the name of Jesus Christ, I order you to get up and walk!" To everyone's astonishment, Peter helped the lame man stand up. The man took a cautious step and then another and then walked straight into the temple to give thanks to God!

Freed by an Angel
(Acts 5)

The Jewish leaders were fed up with the apostles preaching to the people, so they threw the apostles in jail. They wanted people to listen to them—not to the apostles!

During the night an angel freed the apostles. The next morning the guards opened the doors to find the cells empty!

When the apostles were found preaching to the people in the temple, the priests accused them of disobeying their instructions. Peter and the others bravely replied, "We must obey God rather than human beings!" In the end the apostles were released under strict instructions not to talk about Jesus anymore—but, of course, they did!

251

Philip and the Ethiopian
(Acts 8)

Philip was a follower of Jesus. He was called by an angel to travel south on the desert road from Jerusalem. On his way he came across a powerful man—the treasurer to the queen of Ethiopia. The man was traveling home in a fine carriage while reading from the Scriptures, but he couldn't understand what the words meant.

Philip was able to help him. He sat beside the man and explained the Scripture passage, which was about Jesus. Philip went on to tell him all the wonderful news about God's Son.

The official wanted to become a Christian right away, and so Philip baptized him in a river by the roadside that very day!

253

Saul Sees the Light
(Acts 9)

Saul hated all the followers of Jesus. He was prepared to stop at nothing to stamp them out and believed that he was doing what God wanted.

Many fled to Damascus. Saul set off after them, but on the way, a blinding light suddenly flashed down from above! Saul fell to the ground, covering his eyes. Then he heard a voice say, "Saul, why do you keep on persecuting me?"

Saul began trembling. "Who are you, Lord?" he asked humbly.

"I am Jesus," replied the voice. "Get up and go into the city, and you will be told what to do."

Saul struggled to his feet, but when he opened his eyes, he couldn't see a thing!

255

A Changed Man
(Acts 9)

Saul's men led him into the city where he prayed for three days without eating or drinking. Then God sent a disciple named Ananias to him. As soon as Ananias put his hands on Saul's eyes, the blindness was gone!

Saul began to spread the good news about Jesus in the city. People were amazed. They could hardly believe it was the same man! But while his old enemies became his friends, his old friends soon became his enemies! Before long they planned to kill Saul and guarded the gates to the city so that he could not escape.

At night the disciples helped Saul escape by lowering him over the city walls in a basket. Soon Saul (who became known by his Roman name, Paul) began to spread the good news all across the world.

257

A Sheet Full of Animals
(Acts 10)

One day when Peter was praying on the roof under the sun, he fell asleep and had a strange dream.

In his dream a huge white sheet was lowered from heaven. It was filled with all sorts of animals, reptiles, and birds—all creatures that Jews were forbidden to eat because they were considered unclean. Then Peter heard God's voice say, "Get up, Peter. Kill and eat."

Peter protested in horror, saying that he had never eaten anything unclean. The voice replied, "Do not call anything impure that God has made clean."

God was telling Peter that his message was for all the people of the world, not just the Jews!

259

Singing in Prison
(Acts 16)

On one occasion Paul and his friend Silas had been thrown in jail. Instead of sitting there miserably in the stocks, Paul and Silas sang hymns to God and prayed. The other prisoners could hardly believe their ears. Usually the only sounds in the prison were groans and cries of pain!

Suddenly in the night, there was such a violent earthquake that the prison doors flew open, and everyone's chains came loose!

The jailer awoke in a fit of terror, knowing that he would be in trouble if his prisoners escaped, but Paul told him calmly that they were all still there. Then Paul and Silas told the jailer all about Jesus, and on that very night, he and his family became Christians.

261

The Great Fall
(Acts 20)

Paul was in a town called Troas. The Christians there were thrilled to see him. They crowded into an upstairs room to listen as he talked late into the night.

One young man was sitting by the window, hoping the fresh air would keep him awake, but he was very tired, and he dozed off. He plummeted three floors down to the ground! Everyone rushed downstairs only to find him dead.

Paul knelt by the young man and gathered him in his arms. Turning to the crowd, he smiled and said, "Don't worry. He's alive!"

People could hardly believe what had happened and were filled with joy. They went back upstairs, and Paul carried on talking to them until daybreak!

263

Trouble in Jerusalem
(Acts 21-26)

Paul traveled back to Jerusalem. His friends, knowing he would be in danger, begged him not to, but Paul was determined to do as God wanted. He believed God wanted him to go there.

Sure enough, trouble soon flared up. Some people stirred the crowd into a frenzy, and Paul would have been killed had the Roman governor not sent in his soldiers to arrest Paul and take him to the Roman fort.

When the governor learned of a plot to kill Paul, he had him smuggled out of the city under cover of darkness and taken to Caesarea. There Paul was kept under guard for several years before he was finally sent to Rome for his case to be heard by Emperor Caesar.

265

Shipwrecked
(Acts 27)

Paul was traveling on a ship to Rome and soon found himself in the middle of a dreadful storm! For days the ship was at the mercy of the sea. The passengers and crew were filled with terror, but Paul was able to comfort them because God had promised him that they would all reach land alive.

Everyone was thrilled when the coastline came into sight, but then the ship struck a sandbar and ran aground, and the surf began to tear the ship apart!

The centurion in charge ordered those who could swim to swim for land and the others to cling to pieces of the wreckage and float ashore. In this way, they all reached land safely. Everyone on board was saved just as God had promised.

Rome at Last
(Acts 28)

Paul and his companions found themselves on the island of Malta. The rain was pouring down, and they were cold and wet, but they were alive. They spent the harsh winter months on the island before setting sail again for Rome.

In Rome Paul waited for his case to be heard by Caesar. He was allowed to live by himself with a soldier to guard him. Although he was not allowed out, he could have visitors, and in this way he was able to carry on spreading the message to new people. He also had plenty of time to write letters to his friends around the world.

It is not known for sure how Paul died, but many people believe he was executed while in Rome.

269

Paul's Letters
(1 Corinthians 13, 2 Timothy 4)

In Rome Paul wrote to the Christians he had met during his travels. He tried to encourage and help them as they set up new churches.

He told them to be patient, that their suffering would make them stronger, and they would find their true reward in heaven. He warned them to remember what was important, trust in God, and not go back to their old ways because Christ had set them free. He urged them to live good lives and be filled with love and kindness. He said, "Three things will last forever—faith, hope, and love—and the greatest of these is love!"

Before he died he wrote, "I have fought a good fight, I have finished the race, and I have kept the faith." Paul was God's faithful servant to the end of his days.

271